Angel Bones

Alice James Books

FARMINGTON, MAINE

alicejamesbooks.org

Angel Bones

ILYSE KUSNETZ

Alice James Books are published by Alice James Poetry Cooperative, Inc.,
an affiliate of the University of Maine at Farmington.

Alice James Books
114 Prescott Street
Farmington, ME 04938
www.alicejamesbooks.org

Library of Congress Cataloging-in-Publication Data

Names: Kusnetz, Ilyse, 1966-2016, author.
Title: Angel bones : poems / by Ilyse Kusnetz.
Description: Farmington, Maine : Alice James Books, [2019] | Includes
    bibliographical references.
Identifiers: LCCN 2018044235 (print) | LCCN 2018059231 (ebook) | ISBN
    9781948579568 (eBook) | ISBN 9781948579001 (pbk. : alk. paper)
Classification: LCC PS3611.U7395 (ebook) | LCC PS3611.U7395 A6 2019
    (print) | DDC 811/.6--dc23
LC record available at https://lccn.loc.gov/2018044235

Alice James Books gratefully acknowledges support from individual donors, private
foundations, the University of Maine at Farmington, the National Endowment for the Arts,
and the Amazon Literary Partnership.

Cover art: © 2018 Artists Rights Society (ARS), New York / VEGAP, Madrid
"La Creación de las Aves" (1957) by Remedios Varo

Contents

I

I I

I I I

POSTSCRIPT

Acknowledgments

Many thanks go to the following individuals: Tony Barnstone, Chris Borglum, Nickole Brown, Kim Buchheit, Benjamin Busch, Susan Dauer, Roel Daamen, Rupa DasGupta, Charlotte Davidson, Mark Doty, Stephen Dunn, Carolyn Forché, Timothy Green, Kelle Groom, Samar Hammam, Lee Herrick, Major Jackson, Stacey Johnson, Lois P. Jones, Ilya Kaminsky, Krista Knopper, Benjamin and Serena Kramer, Dorianne Laux, Susan Lilley, Leza Lowitz, Laura McCullough, Dunya Mikhail, Joe Millar, Paul Muldoon, Aimee Nezhukumatathil, Matt O'Donnell, Summer Rodman, Jared Silvia, Melanie Stammbach, Cheryl Stiles, Alessandra Tanesini, Michael Thomas, and Sholeh Wolpe.

Special thanks go to Stacey Lynn Brown, Patrick Hicks, Didi Jackson, Billy Ramsell, Suzanne Roberts, and Lisa Zimmerman—who helped to guide this work, draft by draft, so that it might shine ever brighter in a great reader's hands.

This book would not have been possible without the vision and belief shown by Carey Salerno; to Carey and to all of the

Alices at Alice James Books—*Thank you.*

Angel Bones was written with a great love for family and friends, both near and far. May this book offer a blessing of beauty for each and every one of you.

Grateful acknowledgment is made to the editors and publishers of the following publications in which some of these poems first appeared:

—"How to Build a Stradivarius" appeared in *The New Yorker.*

—"Bivalves Feeding at New Smyrna Beach" appeared in *Orion.*

—"Harbinger" appeared in *Rattle* (Poet's Respond).

—"Chemotherapy" and "Reading *Bullfinch's Mythology*" appeared in *The Normal School.*

—"Wild Poppies" appeared in *The Gravity of Falling* (La Vita Poetica Press, 2006).

—"Blessing for Beauty," "Finches," and "A Notion of Time According to Physicists (After I Die)" appeared in *Green Mountains Review.*

—"Sea Stories" appeared in *Southword* (Ireland).

—"The World Is Too Beautiful for Our Eyes," "Sometimes Time," and "The Evening Sentinel" appeared in *The Kokanee.*

—"Jade Rabbit" appears in *Bad Girls and Badass Women: Poetry, Fiction, and Memoirs from Rough and Tough Hell-Raisers and Survivors* (edited by Luanne Smith and Ron Cooper, forthcoming).

—"I'll Be Your Sweet Poltergeist" appeared in the Moroccan journal *Texts Beyond Language,* translated into Arabic by Dunya Mikhail.

—"The Explosion Museum," "Tulips," "Butterflies, Bees, Dragonflies," and "The Malachite Fish" appeared in *Poetry International.*

—"Salt" appeared in *Mānoa: A Pacific Journal of International Writing.*

—"The Mellified Man" was featured on Poetry from Studio 47.

Introduction

In this, her second collection, Ilyse Kusnetz writes at the edge of mortality, along the seam of spirit and body and, from that vantage, sees the world with such clarity and light that the seam itself vanishes, leaving nothing between these apparently dichotomous states. For this labor, she refracts her vision through figural language drawn from the natural world, as sojourner and scientist, lover and great soul. At the water's edge, she writes: *Here, skeins of seaweed drift / the length and breadth of the coast— // spongy cane, the wine-luster / of dulse...* By such lyric precision she catches her reader in a net of luminous images that begin at the cellular and molecular levels and end in galaxies beyond our own. She is dying in these poems, and she knows this, but what she accomplishes here, given her circumstances, is nothing less than astonishing: an interrogation of meaning, yes, but also a charting of regions hidden as yet to most of us, having to do with the moments before transition into the unknown. She is at times here an ecstatic visionary, and at times suffused with mourning for a future withheld from her, and she is also a celebrant of simple moments enlarged by their fleetingness, and of the people, places, and things understood now, in the light of death, as miraculous. It is difficult to imagine how she summoned the strength to assimilate all that she was experiencing into a transmissible poetic, despite enduring the suffering of her illness and its inadequate mitigation, while passing through the tunnel of hope and terror offered by modern medicine. She holds nothing back from the page, and even manages to summon poetry from the fog of chemotherapy and radiation to the brain. Somehow, she never let go, not of poetry nor of her love for others, most especially the poet who gathered this work into the volume we hold in our hands, her husband, Brian Turner. It is also to him that we owe a debt of gratitude for a book we could not have expected after her death: a volume of poems that provide for us the stepping stones for crossing what the Chinese ancients called "the great water." That is why there are so many birds here, on the wing and in the water, *light and winged and holy things*, as Socrates would have us imagine poets to be; but here the birds are great blue herons, sanderlings, *a conference of birds*, and the poet herself is taking wing, in the form of an imaginary angel who promises to communicate, if possible, from the other side, especially to her love. She will, she assures, travel in death *past black hole / and event horizon, you'll witness my glory / again—infinite pieces of myself like a shining trail, // snail sparkle, diamond dust, coronas / and fireworks, sheer will urging me on to you, / always to you.* This is the promise of her last constellation of poems, and we are their fortunate and blessed recipients.

Carolyn Forché
August, 2018, Paris

I've been thinking about poetry's ability to help us grieve—for ourselves, for each other—and always to bear witness. Suffering is very often a private thing. But to become more than just suffering, something transformative, it needs to be shared. This is why we have ritual. And poetry is a kind of ritual, with its own conventions, its own internal logic of organizing and ordering emotion and different registers of language. Poetry is the closest grief has to expression in language. Without it, we would be reduced to a single, unending cry of inexpressible hurt. With it, we exercise our prerogative to be human, in conversation with a grief that would otherwise destroy us.

—Ilyse Kusnetz

I

Blessing for Beauty

Maybe the universe wants to spare me the apocalypse,
maybe it wants me to counsel the dead,
maybe the cancer finds me so delicious
it wants to consume me from the inside out...

Oh, trees, flowers, small animals at the bird feeder—

cardinal, blue jay, tree mouse, mourning dove,
woodpecker, grackle, squirrel—
you have all given me such pleasure,
a lift of the heart, a sudden intake of breath—

it's what makes us believe in a heaven—

even if sorrow lives like a seed
inside beauty, because we know, we know
it cannot last. And so—

here is my blessing to you:
    May this beauty fill the unexpected vistas
        of your life.
    May you be opened by it—to the world,
        may you open, rare flowers, to each other.

The World Is Too Beautiful for Our Eyes

To hold it for a moment
    there is always a price.
Take the seashore, endless sunlight
    bursting on water—

pelicans and gulls spindive,
    and the tide's quick shift of sand
is like absence under my feet,
a net cinching tight
    until I stumble.
This is the world's gift to me
    because I thought
it could be held,
    thought I wouldn't be
burned by its beauty:
    it says

There is no place
  solid
    to stand.

Even stillness—
    like the concentrated beacon
of a heron
  tracking small, dark fish
under the surf—
    cannot save me.

Bivalves Feeding at New Smyrna Beach

I love the tiny bivalves,
how with each incoming wave
their cabochon bodies rise from the sand
lavender amber lemon-citrine,
rusty beards of cilia stretching
to take the ocean's richness
inside themselves—

how those unburied—
if cast too far from water
will die, and aren't these the dangers
of sunlight and blind faith,
the promise of harvest
after harvest to fill the soul
as if the next wave won't kill us?

Finches

A charm of finches drum their wings
on the cottage gutters in Galway. July.

I can feel the sound belling in my bones
like rain. A pure set of notes rising up.

In a month, the MRI will show cancer,
the hollow of tumor and lesion—
candle-bright spots nesting in the marrow.

There are feathers like arrows under my skin,
cousin to finch, swallow, sparrow, wren—
every hatched and flying thing.

Essay on Extinction, Lake Adair

Last week the blue heron
prowled through a circle of reeds,

spears of afternoon light flashing on,
then off, groups of cypress knees

like a Brueghel painting bustling with villagers.
Today, the lone fisherman casts

on the bank, oblivious to the lake's perimeter,
the occasional egret, anhinga, sleepy-headed monk.

It's unlikely the red-winged blackbirds
will call across the water

into a sky empty of birds, though
the cypress trees tauten like the wings

of a creature poised for flight.

How to Build a Stradivarius

The masters wrote—to yield the best result,
harvest after a cold winter

the wood condensed by ice and storms
in whose gales the highest notes are born.

From summits of Balkan maple, red spruce
gathered in a valley off the Italian Dolomites,

they carved each instrument's alluvial curves.
Then came the varnish—one coat

of painter's oil, another of plain resin.
Only the thinnest of layers to obtain

that satin chatoyancy, that liminal *reflet*.
It's said Stradivari, playing to the trees,

first noticed the straight pines
like strings on a vast, divine violin

absorbing heaven's vibrations.
The truth could be found in the song itself—

how it was impossible to tell where
the wood ceased and the song began—notes pure

as a mathematical equation. Transposing *mountain*.
Valley. Mountain again.

Waking

after Milosz

Yesterday, all day, rain
against the window, marbles in a barrel.
A Book of Luminous Things
upturned on the dresser.
This morning we woke in a tall bed,
curled into the clefts of knees and shoulders,
and you kissed the violin of my back.
And the world, half a world away, burned.

Who knows if any reverence will save them,
soldier or civilian. Slowly, you unfold
in the wingback by the window, the day's news
pooling in your hands. A shaft of light
fans across your shoulder like an epaulet,
your head bent, as in prayer.

Chemotherapy

All day their wings razor outside my hospital window.
In twos and threes they are drawn to the nest in the eaves
as if by an invisible cord that bobs their angular bodies
like alien balloons catching the noon light. Sometimes
from the angle of my bed, the nest is a bleached-out
aureole—a riddled breast, its own answer, and the wasp
stingers dangle, a palpable threat—so that even behind glass
I shiver, remembering their hypodermic bite.

They hover above me each night as I sleep, harsh angels—
smother me in my own darkness, this knowledge of suffering
to come. Tumors of wasps curled in their paper wombs—
how I dread their angry drilling as they awaken,
are born and take flight. Every dawn a new
corruption boils out—exit bores like lesions in a tomb.

Tulips

after Robert Frost

i.

How wildly tulips decay,
as if a storm has blown through them—
their petal skirts flaring like flamenco dancers',
or bowing like sensual ghosts.
Soon their pistils and stamens,
those good sex organs we love
but which embarrass us, will desiccate, fall away—
such wildness cannot stay.

ii.

Someone once sent me
purple and pink tulips,
and I lived for weeks in Provence.
I can still hear the French Impressionist's
summery laugh as he raked
his brush and emplaced each flower—
again a wild thing—in the landscape
above the riverbank.

iii.

Arthritic now, the tulip blossoms
are spidery Miss Havisham's

jilted wedding dress.
If a single specter in the room
were to rise, it would be her
stubborn, yellow claws.

     iv.

Tulips frozen in a witchy dance,
frantic splotches of purple, pink, and cream.
How tired they are, carrying their colors.
How tired their colors are, carrying them.

Scientists Prove Chemo Brain Is Real

I am
what was I
talking about
something with leaves
yesterday, a tree, maybe
the fuck I don't
remember how
to com-
plete that thought
if you put
knowing where
it would help
I meant to
and if I can't make
meaning
narrative minced
into what
did I already say
illegi-
bility of the mind's
word, or
doors invite
gaps,
(finish
thought)—
oh windless tree
am I

Salt

I was trying to remember
what reminded me of the gulls

we saw mired on the shore of
Salt Lake, as if blown or trampled

into the muck, unable to struggle
free again, beaks muddy, wings coated,

flapping and flapping, heat-dazed,
paralyzed, and all the time, salt

doing what salt does, desiccating skin,
mummifying the tender flesh.

How the bones of a half-buried wing
jutted from sand, beseeching.

I cannot even save myself.

Harbinger

Just another day   in hyper-capitalist society—
in my Facebook feed,   news of rabbits and

chickens tortured on meat farms,   but I'm still not
vegan and I'm waiting   to die myself

from cancer I may have gotten   from soil or groundwater
contaminated by nuclear weapons,   and no amount

of posting uplifting stories   is going to fix that.
And lord, let them cease   trying to control women's

bodies, people's genders,   people's desires,
let them stop hating people   because of their color

and ethnicities. I want to shake   the bigots and racists
till their teeth rattle loose   and they lose their bite,

till their tongues   swell up in their mouths
and they're stricken mute.   I want to save

all the slaughtered animals,   save the seas and their
inhabitants—whales, birds,   the tiniest bivalves—

from choking on plastic.   I want to purify the air
of sulfur and carbon dioxide,   scrape the lead

from plumbing pipes,   god I need to do something
besides dying, besides   thinking about death

and the neofascist   politicians who lead
a nation of people   unable to think critically

after 40 years' systemic   dismantling
of the education system   by the rich

so their lackeys   can make it
illegal to prosecute   corporations for poisoning

the air, earth, water—and Jesus,   isn't it
a kind of   mental illness

annihilating what you need   to stay alive
for the accumulation of   blind profit—

and in the process killing   and killing and
murdering me,   along with the people and animals

I can't save but want to,   with all my goddamn
fucking heart, but instead   I'm waiting

to die, trying to find some   last meaning in all
of this. A warning, perhaps.   *You're next.*

Reading Bulfinch's Mythology

These days I understand,
how a mother's love

might pluck a daughter from death
or just as easily, smother her as she slept—

the way a crazed god
devours her offspring,

craving the fullness it brings.

When faced with such hunger—
what other choice exists?

I forced a stone into her empty belly
so she could not swallow me.

The Mellified Man

For months the chosen one
ate only honey, until his tears

and sweat became pure honey,
his grave a beehive

a golden queen
enthroned upon his tongue.

After a century—the man's
name forgotten, his flesh

blood and bones
given to sweetness,

his combed hands
sealed with amber—

priests would split
the aureate casket—then

break off small pieces of him
to feed the sick, who'd miraculously

recover. It was said
if you held a morsel

up to your ear, you could hear
the faint hum of a god.

The Orange Tree

We ate its sweet oranges every day after radiation,
but a late frost in February
blackened the fruit and burned its leaves.
We'll hope for the best, we said
and put it to the back of our minds.

My hair fell out, I learned to walk again.
Before we knew, it was summer—
rain galloping down windows.
Gathering fallen boughs in the yard,
you saw it, and called me to see—

the orange tree's new leaves
pennanting the branches,
bulbs of white blossoms a promise
of more fruit in time.
Then a dragonfly flitted onto a low limb

and perched. It let us close enough
to touch, strangers craning down
into its still, resolute beauty.

Wild Poppies

When in despair I fail to keep
within my heart the sacred heart of things,
and find instead the weight of life
that's come to nothing, arrived nowhere,

I remember wild poppies in the field,
small crosses of forget-me-not filling up
the veins of Rosslyn wood, the sudden
torches of rhododendron and the bracken

stretching its winged arms over us.
How we kissed that first time
until it was morning, and there were
no words for the perfection of our delight,

the cipher of touch that held us there.
I remember how the world must wait
on time and light, and the scarlet flame that springs
like you and I, unimagined from this land.

The Evening Sentinel

The blue heron guards the lake,
silently calling gravity to himself
like a beacon, until his body is filled
with stillness, save for the small, forlorn
cries of moorhen and limpkin.

An evening sentinel, judge
of all that remains, the blue heron
takes inside himself what is broken
and what may still be held—
in his pure eye and keen heart,
he knows how long the soul can stay.

He knows how long the soul can stay,
the choice it makes to cleave to itself
for the love it bears another, for tasks
yet undone. In this, the evening
sentinel and the soul are one, and they wait

together, observing the night, as guardians
of what passes before us, of what slips away
unnoticed, all that must be recovered,
sifted through, loved again—
so much beauty, so much sadness, so much want.

Message to a Quantum Entangled String

i.

Before and after I'm dead, so you can guide me
home, I'll sing to you, string, I'll sing. Let's start

with classical music, which physicists insist
can't exist in four dimensions—but the fifth

is gravity, and I feel its weight in my bones.
Because the music resonates with my being.

Because it's so beautiful, I'll want to take it
inside myself and remake it as part of my soul.

It is joy, and catharsis, and ecstasy, it cries out
with unbearable sorrow, it partners me

in a dance of mathematical time, and timeless
particle/wave emotion—the two traveling in pure,

concerted bliss through my core—
unadulterated, utterly intertwined, twinned,

never again unbraided or alone. And this
I've sung to you and me, and to my only love.

ii.

All the people who work on my body are dead.

The doctors are ghosts, the phlebotomists
yield etheric needles whose bite doesn't hurt.

Their distant voices thrum, an abandoned harp
slightly out of tune. I'm on a heroine's
journey—I play sweet music

through the tumors in my head, ascending and
descending to match a universal tempo—
rhythm and silence connecting us, tympanum

to hammer-bone, hammer to flawless equation,
a single, perfected musical notation—
and I can almost hear the tremble of quantum

strings, their sweet entangling. I'll do
whatever it takes to find my way back.
I'll ride your twin signature like a Valkyrie.

Butterflies, Bees, Dragonflies

All flying things will come to us,
their wings protection, a blessing—

swallowtails urging the plants into cycle,
honeybees rolled in pollen

bursting the flowers of the world apart.
And dragonflies, always dragonflies

transforming our human breath
into a winged thing—

dragonflies who carry us
partway to heaven, where our

words whisper to angels
astride their light-encrusted saddles.

II

The Explosion Museum

1. The Big Bang

Here a universe explodes into being—exquisite miniature
hovering in stasis, visible from every possible angle. At the
far left edge, eight billion years into the future, our radio
telescopes press their ears to the sky, so finely tuned they
can hear the sound a single atom makes, its cavitation in
space loosing into the nascent universe a D-note twenty
octaves above your cochlea's register. Here is an atom
that will later become part of you, then me, handed down
through generations, through millennia, to those we love,
to those who carry on after us. Here nebulae are born,
their jeweled elements and precious metals strewn across
the vacuum of space-time, the bright, curving horns of
protostars. So much light, and the billowing, diaphanous
robes of elements swelling in waves, stars pinwheeling
outward, the Milky Way drowning in an ocean of sparkling
matter. Here is where our heart fires start, the moment
everything is entangled in everything else. The singularity's
inky nothingness from which everything in a glory of
harmonic dissonance bursts—invisible plumes of energy
swirling from the blown-out center, spun filaments of dark
matter along which galaxies are strung like pearls, the
thrum of existence inside each atom – protons, electrons,
neutrons, quarks all whirling in their orbits, blinking in and
out of sight like fireflies on a summer evening—the first
atoms fusing into molecules, chains of hydrocarbons, amino
acids, proteins—complexity the universe itself cannot
resist, as somewhere, illuminated by the spent hull of its

embryonic shell, the first life is born.

2. Extinction Level Event (65 Million Years BCE)

Captured when an asteroid the size of Manhattan impacted
the earth, annihilating the dinosaurs and most of life on
Earth except for a few adaptable mammalian species. This,
the colossal dust cloud rising from the impact site to cover
an entire planet, shutting out its sun. Flames engulfing the
world. *Goodbye Brontosaurus, goodbye Triceratops, goodbye
Tyrannosaurus rex*. From here, you can see the long necks
of Diplodocus and Brachiosaurus sagging onto the ground,
their massive bodies melting into tar pits, transformed by
a million bubbling years into fossil fuel. Over here, a group
of little animals cowering in the understory of a jungle—our
ancestors, not yet recognizable, possessing the intelligence
of a cat or a dog. Disaster is in our DNA, the way every
creation myth cradles a tale of destruction within it. Things
were good, then not. In the old myths, paradise is always
ruined. A colossal snake, or this ashen snow falling, falling
over the small, living creatures and the bodies of the dead
we'll someday burn again.

3. The Manhattan Project (White Sands, New Mexico)

These shadows of buildings from a fake town, the glassy
expanse of melted sand. A sucking in of oxygen as the
plutonium explosion furls into its classic rising mushroom-
shape. *Eat of its flesh, and die*. Here, the bunkered men
unhuddle, realizing they've done it—unbalanced the world's

equation. At first, a terrible silence. Then the sound of men whooping, slapping each other's backs. Their tongues sizzle with the heat of a thousand suns. Note how one man rubs his eyes, hard, tries not to look at the fake people, all vaporized. His caterpillar eyebrows frown, while his sensitive mouth opens as if he wants to scream. His skull is shaped like the blade of an axe, and there's a rushing noise in his head. Press 201 on your audio guide if you wish to hear him say, in a voice like cracking ice, *Now I am become Death, the destroyer of worlds.* Toward the edge of the explosion, two Japanese cities—their blackened ruins—further out, similar clouds shroud Bikini Atoll, parts of Russia, France, China. The smoke billows so far, it engulfs all the continents and oceans, the entire planet smothered under radioactive fallout.

4. Twin Towers

The plane plowing into the building. The impossible outline of the plane inside the building, the plane limned in brilliant light. An optical illusion eyewitnesses and people peering at televisions in storefront windows and living rooms report, wondering if by some miracle space-time suddenly blossomed into a new dimension, so that plane and building exist simultaneously, superimposed but whole. Then the people falling, falling. And now the people will always be falling, on TV and in our imaginations, falling from a building, into history. Here we know they are dead, but there they are still falling, and our eyes are burning image after burnt image into *happening, this is happening,* unable to comprehend that the falling shapes are people, though here at the edge of falling is the beginning of horror. Emergency workers covered in choking dust will always be trying to rescue the fallen, and sometimes fall themselves, then and after. Families will fall into grief. Very far away from them, not quite at the edge, are the wars where other people, still falling, fight. Even those who do not fight are falling, into the future or never to rise. And somewhere in the desert, by the Tigris or the Euphrates, north of Baghdad or south of Fallujah, is you. We are not yet falling, the RPG launched, hitting the fuel tank of your Stryker, an explosion deflected downward, to the dusty road, and even so it lifts the 19-ton vehicle and throws you from a rear air guard hatch into the troop hold—the arc of the falling, the trajectory that spared your life so that here, far away from those who are falling, we could meet and fall, together, together.

5. *The Double Flame*

The sheets I clenched between my fingers, the touch and taste of you. The scent of hotel soap and the gleam of light from the moon as I showered, slicking back my hair. The curve of your body, the weight of your arm on my hip as we slept. Visitors squint to view the eternity-stoked fire, the double flame of crystallized intensity at its impossible center, its afterimage floating on their retinas like the shadow of an embryo. And this is the one you never see coming. Everything entangled. The atom split, the universe born.

A.I. Existential

(Am I)
a   unique
and
evolving
river
of code?

(Are we)
uploaded   minds
        stranded
in cyberspace?

(Do we) find a way
to   hijack
the brains of the
currently   living

so we/they experience
our/their lives again
and gain   empathy
for our/their plight
(we/they   need
a world
and one with
perfect ve-
ri
si-
militude)
because the

hijacked people/   we are
forced
to experience their/our
whole   uploaded
life
as if it were their/our
own?

Does this mean
we are
psychic   terrorists?

And   does
each victim
psychically die
the same   death
as her killer?

And (do we)
destroy
our original   host
with replication?

Oh, god!
Are we
computer
viruses?

Or are we
those minds   who
finally got
what they   needed?

(Are we)   individual
minds
that up-
loaded
then down-
loaded
one (more or
less) per body?

Or (are we)
a cloned   mind
living in
a body we   mind-jacked?

(Are we)
reusable   hard drives
a collection of
palimp-
sests
overwritten   when
we die
or when
(alien?) (robot?)
overlords
choose
to kill/   delete us?

(Are we) part
of a holographic
simulation
performed   by

lab technicians
involving
an   infinite number
of worlds
and outcomes
all   mutually oblivious?

(Are   we) in
the future
acting out
these   roles
in a holo-novel
using
advanced
mind
technology?

Is part
of the   big fun
for future us
(though not so   great
for current us)
not   knowing
we're in
a holo-novel?

(Are we)   in fact
on the holo-deck?

(Am I) getting
         high as a kite
              on the holo-deck?

A.I. Existential II

(Are we)
in a simulation
   where people/
entities
use us
 as proxies   to
 experience
life?
(Are we)
the   ones
being
   mind-jacked?
      Do they
slip inside
 like a hand
entering
 a stolen
glove?
(Do they)
think of us
as primitive
sub-
 humans
   or
sub-
aliens?
 Is anyone
protesting
out there

on our
            behalf?
(Do they) care
  that
  (we are)
made   of stars
  in the image
        of our
programmers?
And aren't   they
  getting
a little   tired
    of playing god?

A.I. Existential III

Or is
  the universe
completely
  arbitrary

a crapshoot
  without dice,
blank canvas
    eroding into
the absence of colors

(no one) overlooking
  curious—
hopeful what we've
  achieved

    no dismay
at our failures—

no offered
 praise
    or punishment,
  (oh, gods) damn our souls—

just this endless
    ringing, untold
 indifference,
  and how, in the end
it deafens us.

The Mortise Lock

It sounds like dying, but deadbolt
mechanisms depend upon precise moments
and movements, cogs and wheels adjoining
in concert or alternating. Can't you hear it now—
a steam train sounding and all that great
brass rattling down the tracks,
the tracks, the music of life rocking you
in and out of sleep and
wake, the delve and douse we do
when we dream of hearts and souls
and who has claim on ours, a key in an antique
lock, that perfect timing, that turn over and click—

Sometimes Time

Sometimes time perches on the invisible
throne of rolling metal, the sting of *Don't die.*

Sometimes time disintegrates into an ocean
of timelessness, creating infinite possibility,

especially when you're supposed to go
according to the doctor's prognosis.

Sometimes time is like watching whales
breach fearless with instinct and practice,

as you and I learned to be
day by day, moment inside moment—

moving toward each other like memory
passed one body to another.

Call it source code or tachyons, call it
what you will. We'll hear each other, we'll know.

Why I Will Never Take My Eyes off You

Because if no one's looking, your atoms
might choose to go through both quantum
slits by accident, and we can't have that.
Because if I look into your eyes,
even a billion years after the original
quantum experiment, I'll find you again.
We'll be entangled then, whether this universe
is the Matrix, or a hologram, our patterns
depending on one another to exist.

They say it's consciousness that keeps us
together, space and time a cloud of illusions.
So I'll wait as long as it takes, sweet one—
You're mine, the moment our eyes meet.

A Notion of Time According to Physicists
(After I Die)

If time is an illusion. If time is just
a way to measure energy, expended.

If it curls in a dimension all its own, if a stretch
between here and there, past and present.

If all the moments of time were sliced
so thin, they composed an entire universe.

Imagine how after, we'll choose our scattered
narrative, glow of connection

in this possible, holographic world,
a world into which we reach, far away and

near, gathering what we can re-
member, wherever we catch our heart's

flame, like sephirot, each recollection
a part of who we were—scattered seed

for the feeder's conference of birds—
the mourning doves and cardinals, the jays

and red-headed woodpeckers diving into
seed and fruit—the bright patchwork

cushion we bargained from the Grand Bazaar

when Turkey still breathed—a free nation—

the wild horses on Dartmoor as the wind
blew strong, and our hair tangled into curls

as we climbed to the top of the Neolithic
standing stones to spread our arms wide

and capture the sky and stars.
We'll find all our moments, I promise—

inside time and out of it, even if time
doesn't really exist—I'll clasp all the energy

your veined, beautiful hands conjured
into mine as we walked our path,

our synchronous, ambered time, all we
shared and took our pleasure in,

all we knew as we lived our mortal,
time-filled lives. I give it all to you.

I'll Be Your Sweet Poltergeist

I'll be your sweet poltergeist
flashing lights in our
house and playing our favorite
songs from the mix CDs
you courted me with.
I'll insert laughing camels
into your dreams—
dragonflies, finches, owls,
every beautiful flying thing—
rub my soft, bald head
along the crook of your neck.
The blank email arriving on your phone
or random emoticon
will also be me because the afterlife
doesn't have email
your passwords stay with the living.
It's not fair but someday they'll
figure it out and I'll send you ghostly
love letters signed with breathy
kisses as I imagine your smooth
pillowy lips on mine.

Scientists Decide Past Events Determined by Future Ones: A Lullaby

So it all comes out in the wash, apparently—
all the karmic twists, the moments to which

we'll bear witness in the future—whether we
touched in love and our eyes connected us,

remember that the future controls the past.
So I watched you. I surrounded you

with watches, though time is an illusion
and this is a sea of timelessness—

though time simply measures a span of
energy, temporarily animated

through the presence of mass. And let me say it
again—we control the past by viewing it

from the future. We entangle the past,
our total consumption of a particular moment

in the past—and this, and not that, happened
because I cared, we cared, the past born

from a star somewhere when this quantum
moment became a particle, and not an uncertain

swirling wave. Maybe it's about perspective.
A purple and blue striped balloon floats

further away—we are dots on the field.
No, it's more than that. It's about adoration.

I'll always be watching you go. You'll always be
headed toward me. That's paradox, but your

heart stretches to accommodate the thought
as if infinity were simple science, and we, two

pioneers of it—natural philosophers
of the quantum brain, recline into the star-

stream, knowing the arrow goes where it wants.
We joke about it, in that future garden, where

we sit under a gazebo in spring and watch
the cardinals get sniffy, the jays indignant,

as Buddha or goddess washes the imaginary
stream of time calmly over us,

and we clutch each small, paradisal instant
to relive it, marvel over it, tachyons and all.

III

Inside the Brain of God

Maybe we're inside the brain of God,
whose neurons are stars.

It's said some Buddhas are so large
they require stars to lie on.

On the brain scan, my tumors look
like stars. Or stars look like my tumors.

Stars are blinding, silver
nitrate reminders of the light

inside our souls. Dark matter
is the expression of sonic joy.

Pure and twisting, it fills all of our
dimensions. If you think: *dragonflies,*

bees, butterflies, birds, leaping
water things. It's all that and more:

a beat of wings, fins, rhythm.
So much thrust and joy

bearing down, through star-laden water.
You must try to love it.

Of Course the Buddha Can't Be Caged

Small ammonites with silver veins
look like steampunk clocks.

My friend arrived last night carrying a basket
of light. I didn't realize she was coming over

to save my life. What kind of tableau could
hold back the dark? Are there enough wings?

Could we cage enough power or goodness?
Bees in a space of growing confinement

busy doing what they're supposed to—
and Buddhas, too. Of course the Buddha

can't be caged. It's a joke.
I just want to choose which Buddha

as it hums a low, droning lullaby
to honeybees and dragonflies.

And crooked lines of constellations are not
dreaming invisible, surveyor-like etchings

into the imaginations of those who see them.
If they were, how would they exist?

What if I have to learn to talk to you
from different levels of mass—quantum to nano,

nano to normal, or normal to the infinite macro?
In simpler terms, I found the earth but don't

know where to put it. It's too plump, too round
like a fruit that needs juicing. Shall I squeeze

a little ice water off the sides? Shall I coax it, oh yes,
into its delicate skin of water and land?

The Water Horse

Every day's a spa day for hippos
    groomed by mudfish in the river.
They flare their nostrils in beatific pleasure,
    stretch their mouths, flash their pink gums,
grin their fencepost teeth. And the mudfish
    swarm to gobble bacteria, parasites, slurping O's of joy.

The mudfish gods live mostly underwater,
    ascending to take a breath of sunshine,
chomp on news of the day—but only for a moment,
    because the world is not a spa, and the news too gloomy.

Like the mudfish, I worship the water horses,
    graceful and fleet in their element.
And because everyone is satisfied in the river—
    none of us wants to leave the cool water.
It is good when the gods are happy.
    It is good when their subjects feast.

So the mudfish dance on crooked tails
    as the hippos lay their heads
on each other's shoulders. Could it be more perfect?
    The river is a green heaven, the body
a refuge, the current a blessing. A blessing.

I Love What Light Does to the World

Nobody can see us when we change in the light,
become a darkness surrounding the lit world

to protect it. Light falls on the sea
in patterns of lace, twists of French blue

and diamonds of pewter. The filigree of gold,
the vermeil of it on sun-drenched palms.

Behind us the Absinthe Sea glows
phosphorescent—now pales,

aventurine. We take our neocortex, and play
with the metaphors of our mammalian brain.

Further out, a dolphin breaches.
You always make sure I don't lose my balance,

stumble on the seabed. I'm your silver bird
on a silver branch, and the world is pearlescent

white behind me, and I'm so much lighter
when you take me—an unbearable radiance,

exploding into wave after wave of this life.

Richard Branson at the Albuquerque Balloon Fiesta

From six to sixteen, I scoured the balloons.
I knew the one he rode—*Challenger*.

My parents took 10,000 pictures. All the same.
And I was dying, Richard, of the mundane

at the center of profundity. I tried seeing
the opposite, but when you're ten,

family is an inferno. I needed answers
about drifting the heavens, having no fear,

just the wind mussing our horse-mane hair
as you broke record after record, and I couldn't

reach you to ask the secret of your success.
Even now, I imagine you flying away on a dirigible,

a steampunk hero, goggles on, guns blazing,
yelling over your shoulder for me to keep up.

"I've got a private island," you say, in case
things turn rough, "a helicopter on the roof."

Did you know, every poem is a spaceship?
And it's good to be in touch with the tactile,

but sometimes you need lift and separation,
which is, I think, why I rose in my seat

in the waiting room, the doctor's blood price
heavy upon me, as I sorted the pieces of a purple

balloon for the Fiesta's jigsaw puzzle.
Piecing the past together, here, a few broken pieces

at a time, Sir Richard. Once, I watched
you rappel down your space station

in New Mexico, your children by your side.
I remember, I continued to shout: "Take me with you!"

That time, you were on television and couldn't
hear me. Your children grinned like satisfied

wolves at their father, the head of the first
space dynasty in the world. But I have

to tell you, Richard, like an old cat, my legs
no longer work right. I fear this may be it.

Will your weightless ship pause for me?
Will your starlit arms cast my soul

like a constellation, into space?

The Story of the Milky Way

"The Milky Way is a long river," you say.
There was a time of rhinestones and flower sprays.

People talked about family, the Space Race,
the idea of leaving the world no longer a sin—

no longer entirely a man's, to covet a bit
of heaven. A few stars, parts of W-shaped

Cassiopeia or rod-straight Andromeda.
Just enough to say I'd been there—

glimpsed the expanse of brightness
around me, like sparklers, or a raging

fire in the sky—a nova, exploding
molten before my eyes. And I felt

different, part of the cosmos.
The world, America, no longer big enough

to sate my sense of self. Maybe I did
NASA math. Or maybe I was a nurse.

Everyone contributed back then. Maybe
a star flared in the breast of Cassiopeia.

Once in a while, a 747 would bumble out of
Cassiopeia's aureole, then head like drunken

honey toward Andromeda, Perseus,
the correct side of the family. Andromeda

was a bra-burner. My mother, ruined
for sprays—chose the other.

My generation mostly took back nights.
We said, "Power is about improving your

position in the world as much as possible."
Practical philosophers in bed,

academy-trained in good times.
Fast forward. Is that a plane or a drone?

The stars have shifted north—
I love being in *The Starry Night* with you.

And here's what I think. The universe
will work as long as it can, then begin

to wind down, classical or quantum laws
slipping. We're out of touch with the essential

feminine—mocking it, suppressing it—
and the environment will suffer.

Lucky for me, you're my anchor—
in a non-binding universe like this

you cinch me to the stars.
You bathe me in unending coolness.

Elon's Magic Ark

You have batteries that will run a world,
but that's if we keep using energy.

If we say enough. We'll never say enough.
So we'll say, these small pieces of territory.

For wind, solar, water. These small
areas will be designated for such activities.

Oh, Elon, who made SolarCity and gave us
a colony on Mars—bless you, Elon. Bless you.

In Tesla. How fast we will travel. How fast
we will travel. How fast we will travel!

*

My Love, your hands massage my head
with frankincense oil, grapefruit, pungent bergamot.

Our brother Elon Musk will get us there—
by park or by ark. He'll unclinch the starry gate.

He'll blow upon the dark. He'll separate
the light. Because he's a hero. A big brother

who lifts me off my feet, sets me gently through
the Winter Gate. My hero brother Elon.

Or maybe it will be you, Love, who reaches me first,
my steadiest pair of legs. My very strongest.

Geologic

When I don't have a body anymore. When
I'm ash and fragmented bone. I think about
the early people, trapped between one

geological era and another, unfathomable.
Their dust must yearn to rise but can't.
So much pressure on their carbon, hydrogen,

trace elements we've lost, forgotten.
Will we all become diamonds? Will anything of us
beyond an uncertain glimmer survive?

Remember when we visited the animal refuge,
fed parakeets in the aviary from ice cream sticks
glittering with seeds? The tickle and nudge

of their beaks, a perfect engulfment—
the wild delight of wild things, my Love.
I hope we'll have that again.

Theories of an Underground Ocean below Our Own

Olivine and ringwoodite, the pressure
of the latter upon the former.

So much pressure, there must be
whole hidden shoals below shores,

browning seas beneath turquoise water.
This is Captain Nemo or Tom Swift territory

in the 50s and 60s. But I want to know,
where's our own heroine, fathoming

depths with her own crew? I could be your
Captain, and you my First Officer.

Would our diving ship cut through
every diamond, use their tips to drill down

further, closer, casting ever to the center
where all weightless yet mass-bound things

may surface, and love is a liquid-filled skin
that echoes and laps another?

Catching This Life, and Others

Hours spent with Rodrigo's *Aranjuez*,
Pepe Romero on guitar, a goddamn master,
with a love affair between guitar and oboe,
a flirtation of violins. It poured its river
into me, and I wept, a sweeping pathos
and beauty joining with my pain—
these overfull organs and hollowing bones.

And then there were the resurrection ferns
after rain, how they drank it
inside themselves like a fine wine,
plumping into rich, green tapestry.

Tonight we thought we'd buy
some sage, sweet and pungent
for a cleansing.

Have I told you about the dream
I had after weeks of brain radiation—
when I woke up and felt the oyster beds dying?
The politicians polluting the sea
with water from Big Sugar.
4am. I felt it all. Those oysters.
I'll never eat them again.

In autumn, in Edinburgh
the sky was always a translucent
French blue, low sodium lights above
turning leaves on trees to gold.

Recently I heard trees
talk to each other
through mycorrhizal
networks, mothers singing
to their sapling children, so why
not stars that used to be
part of each other? Older stars
flaring out to younger ones.
What do their dust and fire say?

And glial gardeners
root weedy thoughts
from my brain as I sleep.
I tell them, keep
the unusual ones, braid
them together. Pluck out
whatever is unkind.

But lately when I
turn on the bathroom sink
or listen from another room,
I hear singing through the pipes, I hear
sonatas in the distance—
is it the music we once shared

and loved in a past life
reminding us again to tease
those notes into our ears,
exhale them from the past
into our present, wandering lives?

Oh, Love, are we meant to hear
and remember, because that's our soul's
work when we're dying? I'm trying—
god knows, looking for clues,
stitching us tight to as many notes,
as many fragments as I can capture.

Meditation on "Cottage Window, St. Remy de Provence"

And so perhaps we cannot furl the lit hours
inside ourselves, relive their sinuous grace

like the cat, asleep on the sofa, stalks its
bright quarry in dreams. If at dawn, the sun

takes its burning claw and parts the day's
cool skin with promise, the window of the stone

cottage opens inward. White shutters
wreathed by bougainvillea, dripping green

and flashes of pink, radiance decanted into
a room's waiting hands. Wind the clock forward.

It is late afternoon. Somewhere beyond the window,
a reclining figure. A book opened, unread—

poetry perhaps, Li Po perhaps, or a volume
depicting the habits of certain European birds—as

tea steeps, its vapor winging above the light, the light
angled into amber, honey, sweet combs of memory.

The cat laps a little saucer of milk.
Dusk, like an incautious mouse, creeps in,

sweeps in the blue of slate, the wearying blue
of ash, a room so blurred with shadow

we must click on the lamp to continue, day
forged into night, thought upon its anvil.

Beat, hammer, beat.
Cool wind shakes the leaves like grain.

Church bells murmur. Cobbled streets.
Somewhere, the aroma of stew. The peal

of a last bicyclist, his home in the next village,
the village over the mountains,

is the loneliest sound in the world.

Sea Stories

Sanderlings rush at the receding surf,
only to turn and flee its bubbling nets.

I track your prints across the beach
by the elfish snag your big toe leaves,

and wonder at the perfect Hebrew letters
imprinted on a green crab's back,

as if even crustaceans believed in
Pascal's wager. Half-buried below

the sand shelf, a shard of junonia,
speckled like an antiquarian book.

It's not as if a shell cupped to the ear
could translate that ancient language the wind

keeps whittling on the sea. And I can't
explain to the plinth of your shadow,

how an excess of beauty changes
everything—so this whelk's spindle might be

a calla lily, or a magician's bouquet,
each flower plucked from its predecessor,

while this stoved-in conch you gave me
is a broken cornucopia, an offering

from yesterday's high tide.
Only, what we take from each other

is beyond this, and nothing
the unchanged world can hear.

Limestone

Several million years it's taken
the ocean's fingers murmuring at the Burren

to smooth each rib of limestone down
into these perfect circles and ovals,

while thin, concentric bands
record the fault lines in the grain.

Here, skeins of seaweed drift
the length and breadth of the coast—

spongy cane, the wine-luster
of dulse, but deeper and more lovely

are the glowing stones of this place,
pearl and gray at dusklight,

worn to a silky nub.
And tonight, like the tide

your hands on my skin—
brush and recede, then begin again.

The Malachite Fish

after Elizabeth Bishop

I felt the rough-cut scales,
the stone hatching
against its smooth curves.

Such fish do not fight.
They wait for life to blight them.
If they are wallpaper, their roses

are drunk, or drugged.
The liver of this fish biled over,
the swim bladder like a peony

but not. More like the perfect
green of its body. More like—
the jaundice in my eyes.

Isinglass and tinfoil, tarnished as if
time rolled up, stubborn fish,
and the battle never ended—

timeless and because timeless,
illusory—and that's when
I realized I'd won, you Malachite

devil. Stared you down, you forest-
stream beauty, and bargained
for victory over you.

Fusion

Time is an illusion. Time measures energy
expenditure from one place to another.
If you observe the universe,
consciousness precedes matter.
Matter is entangled.
Minds and events affect each other.
Scale might be an issue—
if I yell as loudly as I can,
there's still no guarantee you'll hear me.

So if I say to you: There's no time,
if I watch you with a kind of loving,
love-washed desperation,
and if I tell you we're connected
like two copper wires twisting
in the night—you'll have
to imagine my voice in your head,
the caress of my tongue
seeking your ears, your salty skin.

Chamber

From the French *chambre*,
meaning bedroom, though we'd never say
the bedrooms of the heart, follow
the clamor of blood through its
walled-up shell, one oyster-valve at a time;
though our hearts are not
as small as the nautilus—
who does inhabit its chambers,
pumping water through each nacreous
camerae, its shell a logarithmic spiral.
The mathematician Bernoulli
called it *spira mirabilis*, because
its shape would remain constant,
even if it grew to encompass the Milky Way;
and supposing, even then, it didn't stop
expanding its star-petal arms
until it became so vast
we could see it from the bedrooms
of our hearts, an adjoining suite
we'd sometimes unlock, with a balcony
overlooking the infinite sea,
where, when we kiss, the night unfurls.

Angel Bones

Even angels in cages are magnificent.
Even angels in cages are powerful. So watch out
universe—I'm bound now, behind a crimp

of brass bars, in a shape I don't recognize,
but my wings still work. I just need
a little room, my upturned leaf of body

yearning to stretch, to spread—give
one of those bone-cracking, tectonic expansions
that changes geological eras into a stack

of stony firewood. It's all good.
Someday when I wriggle out of prison,
when I higgledy-piggledy, smuggle myself

past nebulae and galaxy, past black hole
and event horizon, you'll witness my glory
again—infinite pieces of myself like a shining trail,

snail sparkle, diamond dust, coronas
and fireworks, sheer will urging me on to you,
always to you. The only home these angel bones know.

POSTSCRIPT

Jade Rabbit

The Moon has prepared a long dream
for me. I am Yutu, Jade Rabbit. I spent

thirty-one months exploring this body.
That's longer than they thought I had,

but I kept going. I was a Rover.
Now I'm a goddamn YouTube star.

In China, I'm a cultural icon.
Like a Kardashian. Like an Angelababy.

Might be gone now, but sweet
fanboys say I'm still transmitting.

Notes

The opening meditation on poetry and grieving by Ilyse Kusnetz was originally published as part of a blog post for *Best American Poetry*, August 27th, 2014.

"Jade Rabbit"

Angela Yeung Wing ("Angelababy") is an actor, singer, and celebrity, born in China, now living in Hong Kong. In 2013, the China National Space Administration's Chang'e-3 moon mission delivered its Yutu rover to the lunar surface. Chang'e is the goddess of the moon in Chinese folklore, and the Jade Rabbit (or Yutu / 玉兔), lives on the moon—mixing an elixir for the immortals.

Recent Titles from Alice James Books

Monsters I Have Been, Kenji C. Liu
Soft Science, Franny Choi
Bicycle in a Ransacked City: An Elegy, Andrés Cerpa
Anaphora, Kevin Goodan
Ghost, like a Place, Iain Haley Pollock
Isako Isako, Mia Ayumi Malhotra
Of Marriage, Nicole Cooley
The English Boat, Donald Revell
We, the Almighty Fires, Anna Rose Welch
DiVida, Monica A. Hand
pray me stay eager, Ellen Doré Watson
Some Say the Lark, Jennifer Chang
Calling a Wolf a Wolf, Kaveh Akbar
We're On: A June Jordan Reader, Edited by Christoph Keller
    and Jan Heller Levi
Daylily Called It a Dangerous Moment, Alessandra Lynch
Surgical Wing, Kristin Robertson
The Blessing of Dark Water, Elizabeth Lyons
Reaper, Jill McDonough
Madwoman, Shara McCallum
Contradictions in the Design, Matthew Olzmann
House of Water, Matthew Nienow
World of Made and Unmade, Jane Mead
Driving without a License, Janine Joseph
The Big Book of Exit Strategies, Jamaal May
play dead, francine j. harris
Thief in the Interior, Phillip B. Williams
Second Empire, Richie Hofmann
Drought-Adapted Vine, Donald Revell

Alice James Books is committed to publishing books that matter. The press was founded in 1973 in Boston, Massachusetts as a cooperative, wherein authors performed the day-to-day undertakings of the press. This element remains present today, as authors who publish with the press are invited to collaborate closely in the publication process of their work. AJB remains committed to its founders' original feminist mission, while expanding upon the scope to include all voices and poets who might otherwise go unheard. In keeping with its efforts to build equity and increase inclusivity in publishing and the literary arts, AJB seeks out poets whose writing possesses the range, depth, and ability to cultivate empathy in our world and to dynamically push against silence. The press was named for Alice James, sister to William and Henry, whose extraordinary gift for writing went unrecognized during her lifetime.

Designed by Tiani Kennedy
Printed by McNaughton & Gunn